LEARN TO BE AT PEACE

The Practice of Stillness

ANDREW NORMAN

SLG Press
Convent of the Incarnation Fairacres
Parker Street Oxford OX4 1TB England

www.slgpress.co.uk

LEARN TO BE AT PEACE

The Practice of Stillness

ISBN   978-0-7283-0178-8

ISSN   0307-1405

Printed by:

Will Print   Oxford   England

CONTENTS

Preface

On the last day of a family holiday in Scotland, I was up very early, having a shower before we drove back down to Surrey. I felt fine, and was looking forward to the journey home. But the next thing I remember is coming to on the bathroom floor, having collapsed and been unconscious for half an hour. Surrounded by paramedics trying to revive me, I was soon informed that I had suffered a brain haemorrhage caused by an aneurism. It had, perhaps, always been there and might have burst at any time.

Lying in a hospital bed in those first hours, my wife said that I was holding on to my wedding ring. This I do not remember, but apparently I was turning it slowly round. Rather like the feel of a rosary, perhaps it was a point of contact with materiality as I floated in a strange inner world of detachment, as well as a deep point of reassuring contact with the unconditional mutuality and presence of the other, which is what marriage is all about.

What I do remember, though, is a surprising calmness. 'You just surrendered yourself into our hands', one of the nursing staff said afterwards, 'which is the best thing to do'. Frankly, I've always been scared at the thought of illness and being in hospital. But in that situation it was all OK, and I felt entirely peaceful. Quite soon I was able to reach out and find my rosary, another tangible object to hang on to whilst lying in bed. I sometimes use it to help sustain a daily time of stillness and, there in my pocket, just a touch can remind me that the Holy Spirit continually prays within us.

It was a while before I felt able to pray regularly again. But in those first days in hospital I was at least able to hold on to the rosary. Later I struggled out of bed and walked, somewhat fazed, along the hospital corridor, blinking at the brightness and strangeness of everything. I held my rosary as I walked, and my few steps themselves became a sort of prayer. Soon enough I made it as far as the hospital chapel, and found there, in that busy hospital building, a place of silence. I was then able to keep a time each day for meditation. Not being in the most alert state, however, I was half asleep as soon as I sat down; yet my surface mind continued to produce patterns of thought even more distracting than usual. But what I did sense was that the deep inner calmness I had felt earlier was somehow a product of the regular discipline of stillness. It was an inarticulate reassurance that meditation really had opened access into that level of being where the Holy Spirit dwells.

I felt reassured that, although my attempts to pray always leave so much to be desired, the point is not in our own evaluation of that prayer, but in the wholeness which it helps to develop; a simple and totally personal acceptance of reality as a oneness with oneself.

Back home, I was signed off from my work as a Church of England parish priest for three months. One of the first things I wanted to do was to get back to our own parish weekly meditation group. I had often thought of them as I sat in the hospital chapel, and being with them again in the silence was a great encouragement. My mind whirred on as much as ever, though. I sat and I tried to be quiet, but I still thought almost continuously about tomorrow's meals, letters to write, what the weather might be; on and on... However, what emerged for me was an appreciation that, despite all the distraction, a vital inner work was in hand and that, as my body healed, something even more wonderful was going on. I was often on my own in those quiet days of convalescence, while the family were at work and school, with time to read, rest, enjoy walks in the countryside and, for once, to get on with mundane household tasks quite unhurriedly. I was reminded again of the absolute value of being fully present in the moment and finding there all that is good. Again, it was the daily practice of stillness that encouraged me in this. In hospital, grateful for the care of nurses and doctors and for the companionship of other patients, and then back home, quite overwhelmed by the love and support of so many from church and the local community, what struck me forcibly is that what really matters in this life is people, and our having time for each other, as we learn to give and receive love. This, too, is the purpose of the regular practice of stillness, in slowly liberating us from the insecurity of egoism.

Both in that initial return from unconsciousness and throughout the period of convalescence, I felt that I had touched, and was touching, an inner constancy which is the gift of life in us. The importance of the daily practice was simply and decisively reaffirmed for me: making time to listen, to be open to the Spirit and to know ourselves. So I share these reflections which I wrote during the days of rest and healing.

Andrew Norman

Learn to be at peace

The practice of stillness
for time to listen
and to be open to the Spirit
and to know ourselves

1.

Time to Listen

Walking quickly up the High Street in the town where I live, I often see the young woman with a clipboard. I usually do not feel I have the time, let alone the inclination, for the predictable sales pitch. Just occasionally I fail to stare hard in the other direction and she approaches me. What, then, if she were to ask, 'How do you feel this morning, Sir?' That might stop me in my tracks, for rarely do we have time to pause and consider how we really are. If we pause at all, it is likely to be right at the end of the day, and probably just to relax for a few moments in front of the television. But then, supper finished, our bodies are ready for sleep. It is difficult enough to concentrate on the news headlines, and to stay awake long enough to watch the weather forecast, let alone to summon the concentration to reflect on how we are in ourselves.

Yet, slumped in front of the television, our bodies are already expressing how we are—probably physically weary, perhaps mentally drained, and possibly quite emotionally strained too. Not just the general end-of-the-working-day tiredness, but also the ache in certain muscles, the way in which I sit to be comfortable and the stray thoughts which pass through my mind as I stare somewhat vacantly at the television; they all express 'how I am'. But when my attention is lacking, I have little explicit awareness of all that. I hardly know how or what I really feel.

Our whole lives can be changed if we simply take some time out to give attention to ourselves—and to the here and now. Most of us can remember how, as children, there seemed more joy in living. Was it just that we had no responsibilities then, did not have to work, had no dependants and were not aware of the nasty realities in life that, without warning, jump out and bite us? Or is it that now, as adults, we can no longer easily follow the flow of human existence, so are too distracted to be happy? Certainly, in every human being there is a focal point, a heart, to which if we return, we can know joy. But in fact the heart never really allows us to forget this. In the most pointlessly busy times, and even when things have gone badly awry, the heart reminds us that there is something much better. Yet the way back is such a maze— and there never seems to be time.

How is it that we so lose ourselves? I guess, for a start, because we live in a society which seems to revolve around the principle that satisfaction is not to be found in the status quo. For example, few people now choose a career and stay in it for the whole of their working lives. In most areas of work, change is unrelenting, with a continuous stream of new initiatives—notably in education, where teachers often feel worn down by the increasing demands placed on them. In our relationships, we are less likely to settle with one person, and many of us choose to remain single so that our options are always open. Throughout the world, there is a huge population shift away from rural areas to the big cities, and an urban way of life means that we are out of touch with natural rhythms, such as the rotation of the seasons, so that we constantly have to redesign our own patterns of life to escape ennui. Then, without religion, there may be no sense of ultimate reality, so something has to fill that awful void; for to be alone with your own thoughts in silence, and without any consolation, is to come face to face with despair. As the status quo in our society is rarely felt to be sufficient, we reach out for more. The drive is unrelenting—for more money, better living conditions, and so on; and, on a larger scale, the pursuit of international relationships and global structures which are more favourable for our own economic interests. So it is that we say the right things about caring for the environment, while the itch to continue exploitation of natural resources is hardly checked at all. Contentment is not, in practice, a modern virtue. Anxiety, if not the desire for more, makes us restless, and we no longer feel it is enough to stay comfortably at home as previous generations did, cultivating our own patch, caring for a family and watching the sun rise and set over the good portion that God has allotted us.

We might retain an optimistic view of the future for humankind, hanging on to a confidence that the world will not actually be finished off by weapons of mass destruction, or turned into a hot, barren desert through a failure to curb our environmental irresponsibility. In quieter moments, our hope and trust might be that better instincts will eventually engage with the huge technological capabilities which we have the potential to develop, so as to overcome the incredibly serious problems facing us. Nonetheless, the reverse side to our continuing to pursue this increasingly rapid development is the normalization of constant movement. Sitting still just to be, and to appreciate deeply all that simply is, has become highly counter-cultural.

Furthermore, many of our basic attitudes and much of our behaviour is to be explained as a reaction to that which is unacknowledged in ourselves. The work of Freud, Jung and so many others has contributed to a growth in our understanding of human psychology, which has significantly revealed so much more of this hidden dimension to our being and has opened up the possibility of effective therapy. Psychological insights have thus permeated our culture with some of that vocabulary which is now familiar to us all. We smile and can recognise a 'Freudian slip'. It helps to realize that we do all sometimes 'repress' emotions. But in practice it is still very hard for us to recognize much of the shadow side to ourselves, and it is even more difficult to do anything about it. It is as if we each carry a heavy yet invisible sack on our back. In it is all that we do not like about ourselves, our fears, and that which we feel is unacceptable. Carrying the sack is tiring, which explains the worried look our faces so typically have, but at least all the horrible stuff is stowed safely out of sight. Or it is like a tree growing in a place exposed to a strong prevailing wind. The breezes represent the various influences and expectations exerted on us as we grow up, from parents, peers, and others. Pushed in a particular direction, we accommodate ourselves to the pressure, now from this side, and then from that. The result is a stunted tree, albeit one that survives. Thank goodness for deep roots and for human adaptability. But is this the best there can be? When we see a tall, graceful tree which has been nurtured in ideal conditions, and the upright person of inner nobility, free to be himself or herself, we know it is not. Moreover, keeping part of ourselves hidden away requires some energy. To use another analogy, we are constantly running away from ourselves, and are thus unable to be at rest.

As a society, and as individuals, we continually strain towards something better in the future, instead of being satisfied with what we have now. Paradoxically, we also think back nostalgically to the past, regretting that we seem to have lost that golden age when things were much better, or perhaps just simpler. Yet the deeper truth is that the present moment is already blessed with fullness. 'Now' is like the bead of moisture on the grass-blade. Poised in perfect balance, it glows with light and reflects everything that is around. It contains all meaning and represents all beauty, even though its existence is inherently momentary. Nonetheless, for now it is eternal, since it is what simply is. The blessing of fullness requires our attention. In my days of convalescence it was autumn. Passing a window one day, my wife noticed a large spider's web and drew my attention to it. There it shimmered in the early sunlight, made visible by its covering with dew and quivering in the slight breeze. Together we gazed at it in silence. Such a moment recalls us to the primacy of the present and opens us to its depths. So easily distracted, and with so many preoccupations, our attention is ever elsewhere, but here is enough, and now is fullness. Letting our attention return to its place of rest allows our powers of observation to develop and work as they should. That which we might easily overlook in our distracted state is revealed to have a vibrancy which actually increases our receptivity, the more intently we dwell on it. How wonderful is the person willing to give complete attention when you meet. Not looking elsewhere while you talk, never snatching a glance at the clock, nor ever so slightly glazing over as internal thoughts secretly compete; simply being fully there for another is such a rare gift. Just so, the person who can be at peace in what is, without edging away, is a great blessing to the world and is blessed.

Ironically, the emphasis in western society today is very much on the present, but this goes hand in hand with an anxiety about the future, and amnesia or, at best, nostalgia about past history. A deeper, more contemplative dwelling in the present moment, which is marked both by a total acceptance and an open-eyed wonder, makes the past and the future charged positively, rather than negatively, for us. It does so by revealing that they are actually a part of the present. The 'now' in itself recapitulates that which is past, and is the promise of the future. In a full experience of the present, we know all to be one. Perhaps it is this sense alone which can restore an appreciation of tradition for us today. For it is tradition that holds the resources for meeting our spiritual needs, the urgency of which, despite the decline of religion, we are increasingly aware. Tradition is not just the heritage of past treasures but also a living, concrete connectedness with the future. Then ecological responsibility becomes not just a matter of ensuring there is a world for our grandchildren, but of living fully now in this, our own environment.

Christianity, in common with most of the world's religious traditions, includes the wisdom of making time on a regular basis to be wholly present amidst all that can otherwise superficially preoccupy us. In the gospels we read how Jesus rose early and at times spent whole nights alone in prayer. He sometimes took the group of inner disciples with him, though we also see that the expectations of others were not easily resisted. In Mark's Gospel we hear of Jesus retreating with his disciples to a deserted place. 'For many were coming and going, and they had no leisure even to eat. ... Now many saw them going and recognised them, and they hurried there on foot from all the towns and arrived ahead of them.'[1] Jesus often reassured his listeners that they need not be anxious or fearful, and a spirit of simple acceptance pervades much of the gospels. Deeper than the evident authority over all forms of negativity, and beyond the moral challenge which he sets so personally before each one of us, there is an utter calmness. He does not play on our insecurity, but appeals to that which is best in us, showing us the way to be more fully mature human persons. We are given the example of Mary, who recognised the moment for having time to listen. Her sister Martha was doing necessary household work and no doubt Mary usually helped, but just now, 'Mary has chosen the better part...'[2] Jesus encourages us to have a more receptive attitude, as our worrying can cause us to miss the full value of the present moment. 'So do not worry about tomorrow, for tomorrow will bring worries of its own. Today's trouble is enough for today.'[3]

Jesus himself exemplified the human possibility to be fully at home in ourselves. Only in that state can we face reality. Yet it requires courage. To be at rest, stilling our usual preoccupations even for a few moments, means that we cannot for that time evade certain truths about ourselves. More painfully, we have to relinquish that web of meanings which we spin over what we fear as a void of meaninglessness. When the first Christian monks felt an absolute call to leave the compromises of city life for the silence and

[1] Mark 6: 31, 33.
[2] Luke 10: 42.
[3] Matt. 6: 34.

6

solitude of the desert, they too found it a hard struggle. Yet the same wisdom had to stabilise their daily lives, as Abba Moses in Scete knew and taught: 'Go, sit in your cell and your cell will teach you everything.'[4] In the same way, simple attentiveness is our priority; otherwise we shall never find ourselves. We too need to stay still and to persevere daily in that practice.

Although it is a simple discipline to set aside a few minutes each day just to sit still, many impulses arise to thwart us in the practice. 'This is just silly.' 'A waste of time, and I'm too busy.' 'My mind is too full and I can't switch off.' Circularity may continue in our lives, and become habitual, so that we fear stopping, more and more. It may even take a crisis—something which makes us realize that we just cannot carry on as before—to make us stop. That is the moment of grace. We can start to come home to ourselves.

The practice requires little. Find a quiet place where you do not feel distracted. Sit in a comfortable position, which for most people will be a good supporting chair. The back and neck need to be straight, feet placed flat on the floor, and hands resting, perhaps palms upward, in the lap. Be sure there is no sense of strain anywhere in the body. If there is, then consciously relax. Close the eyes lightly and begin to breathe deeply. Already you will probably be asking: 'What am I trying to achieve?' 'Does this feel right?' 'Is it doing me any good?' But none of that is to the point. The aim of the exercise is to refrain from all self-assertion, and in total simplicity to be at one with all that is. You may be aware of sounds and happenings around you. Just enjoy them. Love them. But do not concentrate on them or anything else. For these few moments, be fully at home, accept your self and accept the environment as it is. Savour that elemental joy which arises from within our depths when we are simply still.

---

[4] *The Sayings of the Desert Fathers*, trans. Sister Benedicta Ward SLG, Cistercian Publications, revised ed. 1984; Abba Moses 6, p. 139.

2.

Open to the Spirit

The influences and attitudes within our society account for our restlessness. So do the inherent dynamics of human psychology. The Christian tradition informs the more fundamental explanation that we are simply incomplete, though already promised the fulfilment which we lack: 'For here we have no lasting city, but we are looking for the city that is to come.'[5] The Revelation to St John includes the great vision of that fullness for which we are being prepared: 'I saw a new heaven and a new earth.'[6] Yet if in this present time we can begin to make a regular discipline of stillness, so as to appreciate contemplatively the fullness of the moment, the here and now, we may truly anticipate that which will come to be. In the midst of all my distraction when meditating, I remember that this is why a contemplative state can never last for long, however disciplined we are. Only momentary glimpses are possible of what shall be. We can perhaps maintain an inner stillness for twenty minutes on a good day, but this always breaks down into the usual anxieties and distractions. So it is encouraging to remember that even the greatest of saints have been unable to prevent daydreams about sex, the next meal, or worries about their health, from interrupting the time of prayer. We should not expect to find continuous peace, 'shalom', in this life. Yet we may look for it, begin to receive it as the most valuable of gifts, and let it be nurtured within us.

But what is wrong with us? What are we lacking? Why can we not already be always at peace? The Christian tradition knows that humankind is 'fallen'. This tragedy of humankind is in Adam and Eve wilfully choosing the way of egotism in disobedience to God. The Book of Genesis expresses

[5] Heb. 13: 14.
[6] Rev. 21: 1.

8

how there is something out of kilter in humankind, which alienates us from God and so from true happiness. The Christian hope of salvation is an opening up of the way to be released from this state of alienation, through Christ's death and resurrection. This assumes a pessimistic view of human nature if it is seen simply as a 'fall' from an original, golden age of life with God in paradise. That may well feed the low self-esteem which is characteristic of the bruised and battered psychological state in which many of us emerge into adulthood. And what empirical basis is there for the idea that a past age of paradisial happiness once existed? What was the great moral crisis of our fall? Were things ever really any better than they are now? Yet the myth of the fall continues to define us as human beings. In a basic, visceral way we all know that, in some fundamental sense, we are not as we should be.

The biblical account of the fall may be applied to our present experience. We can see paradise not just in the past, but as our promised future. Adam and Eve can be seen as ourselves today; spiritually unformed, behaving selfishly because we are immature, like wilful children. Salvation is growing up. As early as the second century, one of the Fathers, St Irenaeus, hinted at such a way of reading the Genesis saga. The Good News is that we do not need to feel bad and permanently guilt-stricken. The Church has played on our susceptibility to this throughout history, and much damage has been done. The authentic gospel never exploits such insecurity, but affirms that, despite all our natural psychological fears and weakness, we are truly loved and valued and safe in the most complete sense possible. The salvation offered by Jesus Christ is, in practice, an encouragement to begin even now to realize the great spiritual potential we have to grow into a relationship with the mystery of God. So finally, in maturity, we may be at one.

9

The practice of stillness is taught in many of the world's religious traditions as the way to develop this potential for spiritual maturity. A closing of the eyes for the time of prayer or meditation may be recommended. But this is so that we may be able to see more clearly. No longer distracted by the sight of those material objects which happen to be before us, we are spiritually open-eyed. The human eye is able to focus on particular objects. I may see a leaf and look at it so as to study all its detail. But I can also stand back and, by relaxing my eye muscles, gaze at the whole tree so as to become aware of all that is included within my field of vision. I no longer need to 'look at' anything. The whole scene impresses itself on me and I can contemplatively participate in it. I see and I delight in the blue of the sky, the passing clouds, the trees swaying in the wind and the flight of birds, but without needing to strain to look at any of them. It is exactly this kind of contemplation which deepens stillness. It involves an opening of our faculties to all that is. There are certainly times when we need to focus on the particular, to read a book, or use the computer, and indeed to be self-analytical about our own behaviour. But it is also a basic human requirement to develop the capacity for simple holistic awareness. For it is in this mode that we learn to be at rest within ourselves and at one with all that is.

3.

Prayer of the Heart

In the Christian tradition the practice of stillness has been referred to as 'contemplation' and 'prayer of the heart'. St Paul urged the Christians in Thessalonica to 'pray without ceasing'.[7] In his Letter to the Romans, he acknowledges encouragingly that while indeed 'we do not know how to pray as we ought', nevertheless, 'the Spirit helps us in our weakness ... for ... that very Spirit intercedes with sighs too deep for words. And God who searches the heart, knows what is the mind of the Spirit, because the Spirit intercedes for the saints according to the will of God'.[8] St Paul realized that the mystery of God is already present within us in our essential being, since 'God's love has been poured into our hearts through the Holy Spirit that has been given to us.'[9] We may think of prayer as our activity, our reaching out to God. But really it can only ever be a work of response and co-operation to that which is already going on. 'When we cry, "Abba! Father!" it is that very Spirit bearing witness with our spirit that we are children of God.'[10]

Yet how in practice are we to co-operate with the Spirit and so experience this prayer of the heart? At the turn of the fourth century a young monk, John Cassian, and his companion travelled far to sit at the feet of the Desert Fathers in the hope of learning an answer to that same question. 'How can we achieve this?' they earnestly asked one Abba Isaac, 'How can we lay hold of it?'[11] Isaac recognised their sincerity and encouraged them, saying, 'Your experience is such that you have touched upon the very central hidden

[7] 1 Thess. 5: 17.
[8] Rom. 8: 26-28.
[9] Rom. 5: 5.
[10] Rom. 8: 15, 16.
[11] *Conferences* (Tenth Conference: On Prayer), John Cassian, 10. IV. 2.

mystery of prayer and have taken some hold of what it really is.'[12] Then he shared with them the teaching 'which has been handed on to us by some of the oldest of the Fathers', and which they continued to treasure so deeply that 'it is something which we hand on to only a very small number of souls eager to know it.'[13] The gem of wisdom which they were given is very small, and yet it has been found, by generations of those similarly seeking such a level of human authenticity, still to be effective. Abba Isaac taught them that to keep 'the thought of God' continually in their minds, they had simply to 'cling totally' to a 'short verse' derived from the Scriptures, and he recommended, 'O God make speed to save me, O Lord make haste to help me'.[14] Though short and simple, such a verse, he explained, because it is of God, 'carries within it all the feelings of which human nature is capable. ... It conveys a sense of our frailty, the assurance of being heard, the confidence in help that is always and everywhere present.'[15] Abba Isaac, however, also emphasised that the verse is not to be 'thought about'. On the contrary, 'This prayer centres on no contemplation of some image or other.' Rather, the word we choose faithfully to repeat, 'to latch onto God in a brief meditation',[16] is an effective way to engage a mind which 'is always on the move'. Keeping 'a firm hold of that little verse ... so that all our ideas should cease to appear',[17] we can then ourselves 'pray without ceasing', for our spirit begins to participate with the ceaseless prayer of the Holy Spirit in our hearts.

John Cassian made this discovery sixteen hundred years ago. In our own time, another monk, John Main, rediscovered

[12] *ibid.*, 10. IX. 1.
[13] *ibid.*, 10. IX. 2.
[14] *ibid.*, 10. X.; Ps. 70: 1.
[15] *ibid.*, 10. X. 3.
[16] *ibid.*, 10. XII.
[17] *ibid.*, 10. XIII. 3.

it when, as a young man employed in the British Colonial Service, something prompted him to go and sit at the feet of a Hindu swami in Malaysia, where his tour of duty had taken him. 'When I first met him,' John Main later wrote, 'I was deeply impressed by his peacefulness and calm wisdom.' The swami taught his young western seeker the practice of meditation twice a day by simply repeating a mantra for twenty to thirty minutes. But in his case, the mantra was to be from his own Christian tradition. 'For the swami the aim of meditation was the coming to awareness of the spirit of the universe who dwells in our hearts and in silence is loving to all.' Some years later, having by then identified his own vocation to be a Christian monk, John Main found that this form of meditation, though he was initially turned away from it by his novice master, was in fact deep within his own tradition.

John Main's recommendations are simple and specific. They can be trusted because they draw on established wisdom, and indeed from more than one religious tradition. His teaching corresponds with what became well-established early on within the Christian faith. What he describes is found, for instance, in the Desert Fathers and Mothers, in John Cassian and in the fourteenth-century English writings known as *The Cloud of Unknowing*. The practice of the Jesus Prayer has also been at the centre of Eastern Orthodox spirituality for many centuries and remains so today. The particular approach taken by John Main is followed by many thousands, and small local meditation groups meet regularly all around the world. His witness is now continued after his death by the World Community for Christian Meditation.

Sit down. Sit still and upright. Close your eyes lightly. Sit relaxed but alert. Silently, interiorly, begin to say a single word. We recommend the prayer-phrase *Maranatha*.[18] Recite

[18] *Maranatha* is made of two Aramaic/Syrian words, meaning, 'our Lord comes' or, 'Lord, come quickly'.

it as four syllables of equal length. Listen to it as you say it, gently but continuously. Do not think or imagine anything —spiritual or otherwise. If thoughts and images come, these are distractions at the time of meditation, so keep returning to simply saying the word. Meditate each morning and evening for between twenty and thirty minutes.[19]

John Main realized that, to be effective, the discipline of meditation has to be specific, and practised with faithful regularity. But it must be plainly said that his particular emphases will not be right for everyone.

Another teacher of this form of spiritual practice is the American Cistercian abbot, Thomas Keating. He calls it 'centering prayer', and, again, this is maintaining stillness through repeating a 'sacred word'.

> Centering prayer elicits a commitment to the goal of inner transformation. It suggests a practical method of entering our 'inner room'; by deliberately letting go of external concerns symbolised by closing our eyes and consenting to the presence and action of God within. Next, a sacred symbol, such as a word from scripture, an inward glance toward God dwelling within, or noticing our breath as a symbol of the Holy Spirit, is introduced silently as a way to maintain our intention to consent to God's presence and action within.

> The only initiative we take during the period of centering prayer is to maintain our intention of consenting to the presence and action of God within. This we do by gently returning to the sacred symbol when we notice we are engaged with thinking some thought, feeling, or bodily sensation. [20]

Then, for some people, it might be best not to use a word at all, but simply to have an awareness of the rhythm of

[19] *The Way of Unknowing*, John Main OSB, Crossroad, 1990, pp. 18-20.
[20] *Open Mind, Open Heart: The Contemplative Dimension of the Gospel*, Thomas Keating OCSO, Continuum, 1994.

breathing, in and out, so to hold and to be steadied. Or a chosen sacred word may come to be used very sparingly indeed. There is, however, a common wisdom in the various specific practices within the Christian tradition to use one of the holy names for God; for example, 'Abba', 'Jesus', or the longer phrase of the Eastern Orthodox, 'Lord Jesus Christ, Son of God, have mercy on me'. For Jesus is always the presence in our prayer, since we believe that in him the dynamic of the human spirit responding to the Spirit of God came to perfect expression. Son of God and Son of Man, he is with us—explicitly so for Christians, and, we may say, implicitly for others—sons and daughters of God as we are. The practice of stillness is truly Christocentric.

> In repeating certain prayers the Christian masters of prayer might be compared to those of the Orient, of India, who repeat various mantras. There is a similarity and a parallel, but one of the main prayers of Christian ascetics is the Jesus prayer, and those who pray it constantly repeat the name of him who was born, lived on earth, was crucified and rose from the dead. The Christocentrism of this important prayer is what distinguishes it from all other forms of meditation and from all mantras; for it produces a meeting, not just a concentration of thought; not simply a plunge into some sort of ocean or abyss of spirituality, but rather a meeting between a person and Jesus Christ, who is above the world and in the world.[21]

The western form of the rosary can also be prayed in a contemplative way. Rather than 'thinking about' each of the mysteries, one can rest within them in a state of simple attentiveness. When we sit to meditate we have to be somewhere, in a room at home, or perhaps a church. The mysteries of the rosary can be appreciated as the particular

[21] Fr Alexander Men (1935-90), Russian Orthodox priest, quoted in *Alexander Men: A Witness for Contemporary Russia (A Man of Our Times)*, Yves Hamant, Oakwood Publications, 1995.

staging places where we can be quiet, an environment in which to be still, rather than as themselves the objects of contemplation. In his book *A Doorway to Silence*, Robert Llewelyn writes of the rosary as 'a way into silent prayer':

> We start with the mind gently enfolded in the words (or it may be resting in one of the mysteries) and very properly they are the focus of our attention. After a while that focus is likely to begin to disappear from consciousness, and this is where the beginner may become alarmed. What is happening, however, is that—so long as the intention to pray remains—the heart is being drawn gently into the silence beyond the words.[22]

It is the regular discipline of practising stillness that matters. John Main was surely right always to insist that we need to concentrate on remaining utterly faithful to our daily meditation. But the point of the discipline is to live meditatively, and with a contemplative awareness in all things. It should never bother us if there is just no opportunity to meditate. Meditation should have taught us to accept the goodness and fullness of each present moment with a radical simplicity of spirit, whatever the circumstances. This inner freedom, moreover, can allow us to refresh our usual practice by sometimes going about it in a different way. So the posture of sitting to meditate can be complemented by sometimes taking the opportunity to meditate whilst walking. This might be a good change to make when we have a little more time, on holiday for example. Charles Brandt wrote helpfully, from his experience as a hermit living in a Canadian forest, about this way to practise stillness.

> It is early morning with its quiet and coolness. I walk out the old logging road to Catherwood Road. Catherwood is my connector to the outside world. My hermitage is located deep

---

[22] *A Doorway to Silence: The Contemplative Use of the Rosary*, Robert Llewelyn, Darton Longman and Todd, 1986, p. x.

in the temperate rain forest, on the Oyster River, British Columbia. The logging road along with other trails through the forest is where I practise walking meditation. I do not think of the road as leading anywhere. It is the road to nowhere, the path on which I journey and have been journeying for a lifetime. When I walk this road I have no destination, no timetable or estimated time of arrival. I simply place one foot in front of the other, let all my cares, anguish, angst, fears drop away. My breathing is in harmony with the rhythm of the universe. And although this is the path of nowhere, in reality it is the way to everywhere, because it enables me to enter into communion with the whole community of beings, beings which are diverse, interiorised, and each in communion with every other being in the universe. I become present to the most distant star, and she to me, the 'complicated web of interdependent relationships'. Every atom of my being is present to every atom in the universe, and they to it.[23]

Circumstances and our own disposition will guide us to the particular form of practice which is best for each day. A right moment will come to take up a specific discipline, then to stay faithful to it. Indeed many people have finally come back to meditation a long while after first trying it.

As time is set aside for stillness day by day, so joy will arise from deep within us. Inevitably, though, this will be overcome all too soon by the return of unease, which may be acute at times. We may well feel that we no longer want to carry on, that we just cannot. Silence can be quite unendurable. Before we reach that point, though, we will probably have been filling the silence with our own comforting thoughts. These may consist of genuine spiritual insights, good in themselves. There may also have been a constant stream of apparently quite irrelevant daydreams. We imagine then that we are failing in the attempt to meditate and we may begin to wonder if there might not be some better way to spend the

[23] *Self and Environment: On Retreat with Charles Brandt*, Continuum, 2000.

time. But, if we wish to enter into joy, we have to accept that pain from which we naturally turn aside. For the practice of stillness is the way of the Cross. It may be approached as a technique for achieving self-fulfilment, but the gospel is that the fullness of life can only be received if we are willing to die to self. It is a way, a personal journey, along which we can expect to make progress only at the pace which is actually possible for us. This means that we must be patient and gentle with ourselves. How many people give up serious prayer because they are cross with themselves at apparently being quite unable to deal with the continuous distractions? Well, that's how we are. The mind is constantly active because it needs to be: living in this world, we experience a lot of data that continually has to be processed. But the mind can also learn a deeper form of apprehension, and this learning is always a gradual process. Indeed the 'distractions' may themselves simply be accepted as the present matter of our prayer, to be taken wholly seriously, yet ever and again passed through, so as to be held in the stillness of the deep-continuum.

4.

Letting Go of the Self

We all tend to be egoistic, because we are still 'growing up'. While we quickly become physically mature, just a little personal insight reveals how much longer our psychological maturing requires. Spiritual wholeness includes all of ourselves, unto the very heart (which is our essential identity in the sight of God). To enter fully into the heart is the point of our lives. Yet this goal is for now beyond our self-understanding. We are just spiritual infants being invited to step out into the unknown of growth and learning. Feeling uncertain and insecure, we continually reach back to cling on to some kind of support. Such selfishness, while under-standable, does us (and others) no good. The imperative is to let ourselves be weaned slowly off this natural self-centredness. There is perhaps nothing more important, no greater priority in our lives. In the daily practice of stillness we learn not to rely on ourselves, on our thoughts and on our feelings, but instead to rest in the darkness—and perhaps in the apparently complete emptiness—of the magnanimity of the Holy Spirit who gently opens us out into that greater generosity. Its fruit is simply love. It is our personal response to the mystery of God, made known to us in the person of Jesus Christ, for our maturing into full personhood.

However, even good religious disciplines can themselves become egoistic. We need to remember that the only test of whether they are real and worthwhile is if they make us more loving and less egoistic. In John Main's short and simple yet profound book, *Word Into Silence*, he shows how meditation can engage with the particular forms of egoism that so condition attitudes and behaviour today, no doubt often without our realising it.

> Saying the mantra is a discipline which helps us to transcend all the limitations of our narrow and isolated self-obsession.

... Self-renunciation is not an experience with which our contemporaries are familiar or which they even understand very clearly, mainly because the tendency of our society is to emphasize the importance of self-promotion, self-preservation, self-projection. ... These aspects of our self are illusory; they become little egos when we isolate them from the central point of our being where our irreducible selfhood exists in complete harmony with the Other, the Other being the source of our being and the sustainer of our selfhood. ... This is what Niebuhr means when he said: 'The self does not realize itself fully when self-realization is the conscious aim.' In meditating we affirm ourselves by becoming still, by becoming silent, we allow the reality of our real self to become more and more apparent; we allow its light to diffuse throughout our being in the course of the natural process of spiritual growth.[24]

The practice of stillness is letting go. In relinquishing our desire to think, we are refraining from imposing meaning. This means that we can be more open to the way things actually are. Although there can be no meaningful experience before we interpret the data our senses receive, there can be a certain pause before we do. Interpreting happens along with the receiving of all data, but we can still imagine suspending the interpretation so as simply to savour that data and to wonder. A moment when we turn over in our hands a stone just picked up represents the state of preliminary receptiveness which is so important if we are to cultivate the deeper intuitive knowing of spiritual truths. Wonder is the necessary check to the tendency for reductionism which characterises both religious and secular forms of knowledge. It is as much an unwarranted prejudice to assume that there is no truth in anything which does not correspond with the religious tradition which is mine, as it is to accept as true only that which comes through empirical experience. Silencing the mind, and then getting used to staying with that silence on a regular basis, makes

[24] *Word into Silence*, John Main OSB, Canterbury Press, 2006, pp. 55-56.

for greater openness to mystery. Surely this basic humility is required in scientific investigation just as much as in theology?

It dawned on me during my convalescence that letting go means allowing ourselves to be vulnerable to realities which may shape us, and it will perhaps open us to the chaos we fear so much. We may feel it is safer and more comforting to place earphones over our heads, for our own choice of music to blot out all else. The winds of elemental forces in this universe, the earthquakes of unpredictable disaster, and the scorchings of human suffering, are all too frightening to let the thought of them anywhere near us. Yet when the prophet Elijah resisted our human tendency for evasion and asked to see God, the divine was then manifested to him not in the wind, the earthquake, or the fire, but in 'a sound of sheer silence'. As with Elijah, it is only then that we stand at the entrance to full living: 'When Elijah heard it, he wrapped his face in his mantle and went out and stood at the entrance of the cave.'[25] Finally, this requires us to face our fear that death will be the extinction of the self. That requires the ultimate act of trust and Christian faith. However unwilling we might be to 'go gentle into that dark night',[26] faith is to surrender ourselves even now into that which, then, we shall no longer be able to control. Faith is the letting go into an unknown which will be a birthing more awe-full and more fully life-giving than our first ejection from the womb into the light of day.

As the way of the Cross, the practice of stillness points us along the way of magnanimity, to live in a self-giving way with generous attitudes. Step by step, gradually turning aside from the desire for self-advancement, we then become free to live for others. Literally silencing our self-assertiveness, we are free to be ourselves, and we can then be free to 'be there' for others.

[25] 1 Kgs. 19: 11-13.
[26] From a poem written in 1951 by Dylan Thomas (1914-53) for his dying father.

5.

To Know Ourselves

Just occasionally we might suddenly hear ourselves as we speak to another person, though for most of us this happens all too rarely. Then we may hear the unfair judgement, petty complaint, or note of moral blackmail that so easily creeps into our speech. It may indeed be hard and shameful to listen to ourselves in this way. Yet we are often even less willing to listen carefully to what we are saying to ourselves. The force within us which pushes out of sight that which we feel is unacceptable, or which hides away some deep hurt, has a secret voice and it speaks imperiously, forever telling us what to do. However, just as we can listen to ourselves when we speak to others and realize then what is going on, so we can also listen to this inner voice and learn what it is doing to us.

In stillness, we enter into a state which makes that listening more possible. So many of our distractions, which seem to spoil the time of meditation, are in fact this inner voice as it speaks. Meditation itself is not the time to listen, but meditating can help us to hear the voice, as its promptings dictate our behaviour during our ordinary daily lives. Then, inwardly quieter, we can begin to notice that which rules us. Just as you can only meditate consistently and fruitfully if you commit yourself to the specific practice, so the insight required for self-listening needs to be cultivated through making use of some particular appropriate resource. This may be in sessions with a professional psychoanalyst or counsellor.

One popular technique that has come to be much used in many of the Churches is the Enneagram. This consists of a spiritual template corresponding to typical attitudes and patterns of behaviour. The initial application of the Enneagram can be quite dramatic, when we suddenly see ourselves as in a mirror and with more psychological insight than ever before. The realization that this is how we really are may then prompt a surge of good intentions for personal change. 'Enneagram' means literally 'nine pointed picture'. The nine points of the diagram refer to personality types by which individuals may be identified. It can be an effective working method, because it emphasises the typical characteristics and only then attends to the subtler distinctions. To use the Enneagram, one might read in an introductory manual a series of paragraphs, each of which describe a particular personality type. The paragraph which rings true is then the first stage in identifying one's own personality. A better introduction is made with the help of another person who understands this method and is experienced in its use. Many people begin by attending a residential Enneagram weekend, rather like a retreat, and often this is best. From that stage it is then possible to go on and recognise the finer tunings of our personality in four connected types. Two of these are the wings, which are on either side of our dominant type, both therefore having some influence.

The Enneagram is built around the fact that human behaviour is dynamic. We feel and behave differently according to circumstances, varying from feeling stressed and under pressure, to being relaxed and at ease. Thus the other two connected types are the stress type, which we move into when demands are being imposed upon us, and the security type, when we are secure (though we may also move into that mode, in an extreme form, when we are overwhelmed or exhausted). The nine pointed diagram helps us to discern how we swing from one mode to another in our daily life.

Whether or not the wisdom of the Enneagram really does have ancient roots, it can certainly be a valuable spiritual resource. It incorporates many insights about human behaviour and, when the template engages, it may be with a dramatic sense of, 'but that is so true for me!'. Yet it is only a technique. It may not work for everyone. However, its use can promote personal growth, and with the awareness that this growth is rarely simply a linear progression, but more like a helix. We circle around, and respond to, circumstances which are themselves ongoing, according to our own inner elasticity.

The Enneagram, like other tools for personal growth, allows us to hear the commanding voice with which we speak within ourselves, and also the voice in which we address others. The effect of this can be powerful. 'How awful that I should have spoken to her like that.' 'No, this is really not what I want for myself.' 'This is not good for me.' 'It is not necessary to demand that—but, oh dear, I can now see how I did.' Then it is possible to create a space for a closer listening to ourselves. The regular practice of stillness can encourage this and sustain the courage it requires. As our self-esteem slowly but surely depends less on a false ego which we promote for reasons of self-justification, and more on the mystery of that love which brought us into being and which continues to sustain us, we can begin to face the truth about ourselves and the way we treat others. Using the Enneagram opens our eyes to the working of our accustomed attitudes. That insight can be maintained while we continue to listen to ourselves with the interior detachment which a regular practice of stillness helps to keep open.

Christians may feel that they should not seek happiness, but rather accept the suffering which comes with selfless living. To meditate is to be weaned away from the egotism of our lesser maturity, and this is certainly the way of the Cross. Learning not to idolise our own wants, we are indeed more vulnerable to others. But if we are treated badly, we shall be more able to respond with love. Though we shall still be hurt, and even more deeply so with the self-protective defences lowered, it is much less likely that we shall be left with a crippling burden of bitterness and resentment. To live more contemplatively, resting and delighting in the fullness and sufficiency of the present moment, is to be more able to accept anything that happens. A sudden road accident, the discovery of cancer, or a terrible bereavement will be no less attended by pain, loss and profound frustration. But in and through the human-ness of our hurting will be the way of peace and healing. 'Happiness' in itself is not what we should seek. Indeed, the ego, when it has everything it thinks it wants, is then locked into a rejection of the pain entailed in further maturing, and cannot be truly 'happy'. Joy is the infinitely better gift we receive and, to the extent that we can give away our selves, then truly we shall find ourselves.

6.

The Quest for Stillness

I continue to struggle to maintain the daily time of meditation, and my head soon begins to slip from its straight attentive posture, as the mind clouds over with all sorts of compelling thoughts. But in one sense this does not matter. We need not lose heart. Time and again we can simply return to an inner wakefulness so to concentrate on the repeated word, or rhythm of the prayer. For however prone to daydreaming we are, the constant stream of the Holy Spirit's prayer within us is unaffected. The invitation for us to enter into the joy of our Lord issues from an infinitude of loving patience. Distracting thoughts are just the clouds which pass over the sky. We need not worry about them, for the sun always shines above and will eventually break through. Indeed, the sun literally shines through the thickest clouds, and that thought might encourage us in our meditating.

One of the dangers in meditation is that it may be taken up as an evasion of reality. Yet with faithful perseverance, it will be exactly the opposite. At first, aware of our lack of inner resolution, we may be looking for a way superficially to cover over the void. But if meditation is merely a reverie, a conjuring up of pleasing feelings of calmness and serenity, then something synthetic is being substituted for genuine stillness. The truth is that restlessness born of the sense of incompleteness is an inherent quality of the human condition. In his poem 'The Pulley', George Herbert described this in terms of how God deliberately refrains from pouring into us everything contained in the glass of blessings. Strength is given generously, then beauty, wisdom, honour and pleasure, but the Creator refrains from adding that treasure which lay at the bottom of the glass—restfulness. We must in one sense remain restless, but for our good, since it is this restlessness which prompts us to look for the source of all peace, the mystery of God.

> ... let him keep the rest,
> But keep them with repining restlesnesse:
> Let him be rich and wearie, that at least,
> If goodnesse leade him not, yet wearinesse
> May tosse him to my breast.[27]

That stillness is never our own achievement, but always a participation in the only true and complete stillness which really exists, the Mystery of God. It is precisely in acknowledging our inevitable restlessness that we can be open to its completeness.

So, on a practical level, we need to be gentle with ourselves. At first we may wonder whether we could ever be self-disciplined enough to maintain a routine of spiritual practice on a regular basis. It may seem a tall order. Yet I find myself sitting at the table to eat at least twice most days, and meditating can also be the most natural of daily rhythms. There will inevitably be days, however, when a time of silence on our own is hardly possible at all. We need not worry then, but should just return to being faithful to our commitment at the next available opportunity and resume its rhythm. The point is not so much to meditate as to live meditatively, contemplatively, with the eyes of our whole human nature fully open to all that is. As the saints remind us, prayer is not real prayer when we are aware of praying. So the daily discipline, important as it is, needs to be more and more integrated and assimilated into the whole of our living.

Consciously practising stillness from day to day can truly help us to be more ourselves. It has helped countless millions, both in the Christian tradition and in the wisdom context of other traditions. It enables us to have time to listen, which is

---

[27] *The Works of George Herbert*, ed. F. E. Hutchinson, Clarendon Press 1941, p. 160.

so necessary if our constant tendency to evade reality is not finally to overwhelm us; to be open to the Spirit and begin to appreciate how full of wonders this life is, here and now; and thereby to discern the way for growing into greater maturity. A willingness to make time for this is vital in the world today. So many people are permanently in a rush, despising the treadmill, yet fearing to step off it. So many attitudes and actions, from politics to those within our personal relationships, arise unreflectively and in reaction. In my hospital bed it came forcefully to me that we forget how our lives always hang by a thread. Now is the time to listen for that which really matters, and 'now' is the sacrament of God.

'Learn to be at peace and thousands around you will find salvation.'[28]

[28] St Seraphim of Sarov.